THE FILIPINOS IN AMERICA

THE FILIPINOS
IN AMERICA

Frank H. Winter

Lerner Publications Company · Minneapolis

To my wife, Dulce

Library of Congress Cataloging-in-Publication Data

Winter, Frank H.
  The Filipinos in America.

  (The In America series)
  Includes index.
  Summary: Surveys Filipino immigration to the
United States and discusses the contributions made
by Filipinos to various areas of American life.
  1. Filipino Americans—Juvenile literature.
[1. Filipino Americans] I. Title.   II. Series.
E184.F4W56   1988   973'.049921   88-613
ISBN 0-8225-0237-2 (lib. bdg.)
ISBN 0-8225-1035-9 (pbk.)

Manufactured in the United States of America

1 2 3 4 5 6 7 8 9 10 97 96 95 94 93 92 91 90 89 88

CONTENTS

1
THE LAND AND PEOPLE OF THE PHILIPPINES

Tropical fruits flourish in the hot, humid climate of the Philippine archipelago.

The Archipelago

The Philippines is a rugged 1,000-mile-long archipelago, or group of islands, in the western Pacific Ocean. It is made up of 7,100 islands, which stretch between Taiwan in the north and Indonesia in the south. Most of the population lives on the 11 largest islands. The capital city of Manila is located on Luzon, the largest and most northern of the Philippine islands.

Because the Philippine archipelago is volcanic in origin, most of the islands are mountainous. Since the archipelago lies in the tropics, the climate is very hot and the land green with lush vegetation. The Philippines is located close to the Asian mainland, and this geographic position has played a major role in the history of the country (known also as The Philippine Islands).

Mayon Volcano is one of the many active volcanos in the Philippines. Located on the island of Luzon, this cone-shaped mountain rises almost 8,000 feet (2,400 meters) above the surrounding countryside.

The People

The people of the Philippines are called Filipinos (also spelled Pilipinos), and their country is the only nation in Asia that is predominantly Christian and English-speaking. The Filipinos speak English because the country was a colony of the United States from 1898 to 1946. Some 80 other languages and dialects are also spoken, with Tagalog (also called Pilipino) being the closest to a national tongue.

It is very common for Filipinos to speak two or even three languages—their own dialect, Tagalog, and English, which is taught in all the schools beyond the second grade. Even though many people and places have Spanish names, Spanish is spoken by only a small number of Filipinos because it was used exclusively by the upper classes during the period when Spain controlled the islands (1565 to 1898).

PHILIPPINES

Due to more than 400 years of rule by Catholic Spain, the Philippine population is about 85 percent Roman Catholic. About 5 percent of Filipinos are Muslims, or followers of Islam, a result of contact with Arab and other Muslim traders who frequented the islands, particularly the southern part of the archipelago, during the 14th and 15th centuries. Today there are many Muslim mosques, or temples, on the big southern island of Mindanao. The remaining 10 percent of the Philippine population are Buddhists or members of small Christian churches.

The Filipino people are a varied group, as you can see. One thing is clear: the Philippines is an Asian "melting pot."

Pre-Hispanic Times

People may have first lived in the Philippines half a million years ago. Stone tools and signs of cooking fires dating to that time have been found on Palawan and other islands. The earliest human remains, discovered on Luzon, date to 250,000 years ago. During the last ice age, which began about 1.5 million years ago, primitive hunters probably came to the Philippines from China and the Malayan archipelago. They crossed over natural land bridges that existed because the waters around the islands were more than 150 feet (45 meters) lower than today.

Other migrations used overland routes too. About 25,000 to 30,000 years ago, a small-statured people reached the Philippines from the south. Good hunters who used well-made arrows and darts, they were the ancestors of the Negritos, who today inhabit remote rain forests in northern Luzon. Later migrants came from Borneo 12,000 to 15,000 years ago. These people knew how to use blowguns and to grow crops in forest clearings. They built houses from tree branches and the large banana leaves so abundant in the Philippines and made fire by rubbing two sticks together until the friction ignited dry grass.

When the ice age ended about 10,000 years ago, the land bridges linking the Philippines to the rest of Asia were submerged by the rising waters caused by the melting of the great ice sheets. The first seafaring migrants to the islands were Neolithic (New Stone Age) Indonesians, who arrived 5,000 to 6,000 years ago. Using polished axes, chisels, and other stone tools, they lived by hunting, fishing, trapping, and farming. Large groups of immigrants also came from what is now southern China and Vietnam.

The most important of the new-comers to the Philippines were the Malays, who began arriving from the Malayan archipelago in about 1500 B.C. Either this first group or a later wave of Malays constructed the fantastic irrigated rice terraces along the mountain slopes in northern Luzon. The

These rice terraces on Luzon are more than 2,000 years old. They are irrigated by a system of bamboo tubes fed by natural waterfalls.

terraces are considered one of the wonders of the world.

Iron Age Malays from Borneo came to the islands between 300 and 200 B.C. These brown-skinned people with straight black hair are the ancestors of about one-third of present-day Filipinos. Indeed, much of Filipino culture, including the Tagalog language, has Malay roots. Malays introduced iron, glass, the art of weaving, and the use of carabao (water buffalo), now the traditional draft animal of the Philippines. They also brought a written language. Malay migrant waves continued up to the 15th century A.D.

In the seventh century, the powerful Buddhist empire of Sri Vijaya arose in the Malayan archipelago, with its capital at Palembang, Sumatra. The Philippines came under the sway of this kingdom, which dominated trade in Southeast Asia for some 500 years. Sri Vijaya gave its name to the central Philippine island group called the Visayas.

The influence of Sri Vijaya in turn gave way to that of a new empire, Majapahit, founded in 1293 by Raden Widjay of Java. Majapahit governors in the Philippines were called "sealords" because they used ships and troops to maintain order and collect taxes. The Majapahits were Hindus, but to help keep peace in the empire, the sealords were prohibited from interfering with the native religious beliefs of the Filipinos, most of whom worshipped gods of nature. Neverthe-less, many facets of the Majahapit Hindu culture were absorbed. Hindu culture was also spread by traders coming from as far away as India. For example, the traditional Filipino man's shirt called the *barong* traces its origin to the *kurta* of southern India. Sanskrit words were also added to the Filipino vocabulary.

During the first part of the Majapahit rule, or perhaps even earlier, the Chinese introduced their culture to the Philippines. Chinese trade with the Philippine Islands was so vigorous during the Ming dynasty (1368-1644) that Chinese colonies sprang up in many places. For example, the port of Lingayen on the island of Luzon was named after a Chinese trader, Lin Gai-yen. Fine Chinese silks, elegant Ming porcelains, and other goods were prized by the Filipinos, who traded Philippine pearls, shells, mats, and wax for them. The Chinese empire and culture were so respected that for a brief time, between 1372 and 1421, the Chinese were allowed to govern parts of the islands. Eventually, however, competition from Arab traders forced them out.

Abu Ali was perhaps the first Arab trader to visit the Philippines, arriving in 977. By the 14th century, the islands benefited from being a natural cross-roads between Arab and Chinese trade. In addition to channeling goods and currency into the archipelago, the Arabs spread the Muslim religion, Islam. About 1380, the Arabian scholar

A mosque on the island of Mindanao, where many Muslims still live today

Mudum (or Mahdum) arrived in the southern islands of the Sulu group and began preaching the Muslim faith. A decade later, much of Sulu was converted.

Other preachers eventually came, and by the mid-15th century, Islam was firmly established throughout the Sulu archipelago, in Mindanao, and in Borneo. When the Spanish arrived in the early 16th century, they found the once-great Majapahit empire in its last days and Muslim footholds established on Luzon.

Magellan's Voyage

On March 16, 1521, the Catholic feast day of St. Lazarus, three Spanish galleons sailed toward what appeared to be the end of a large island in the

The explorer Ferdinand Magellan made the official European discovery of the Philippine archipelago.

western Pacific. The three vessels, under the command of Portuguese-born Captain Ferdinand Magellan, had reached the southern end of the island of Samar. Magellan named the island St. Lazarus. It was the official European discovery of the archipelago later called the Philippines.

Not often mentioned in history books, however, is a trip Magellan had made nine years before. In 1512, he had set sail on a secret exploratory voyage from Malacca in Malaya and apparently had then first set eyes on the Philippines. He may have visited the Chinese settlement of Paria on Luzon and cruised around the archipelago. Magellan was evidently amazed at the gold mines and precious pearls of Luzon and made up his mind to return.

The official reason for Magellan's later expedition to the Pacific, which began in 1519, was to seek a shorter, westward route to the Moluccas, or Spice Islands, which are now part of Indonesia. These islands got their name from the exotic spices that grew there and that were almost as highly treasured by the Europeans as gold. Spices were prized for cooking and brought fabulous prices in European markets. But Magellan's native Portugal did not support his plan to find a westward passage to the Moluccas. Frustrated, he renounced his citizenship and was then successful in getting both Spanish ships and support for the dangerous expedition.

Magellan's long westward voyage took him south from Spain, through the straits at the tip of South America (now named in his honor), and then across the wide Pacific. After reaching Guam on March 6, 1521, he continued his journey and landed on a small, uninhabited island in the Philippine

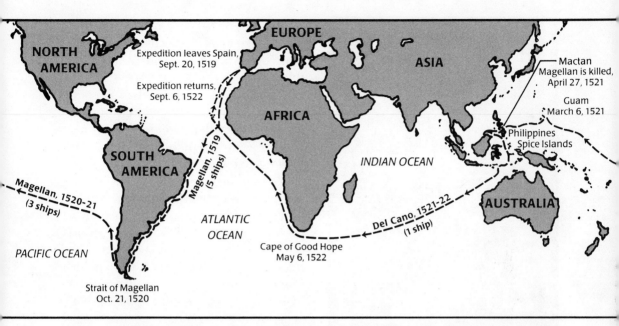

The expedition led by Captain Ferdinand Magellan made the first voyage around the world. Magellan himself was killed in the Philippines, and the single ship that returned to Spain at the end of the three-year voyage was captained by another member of the expedition.

archipelago. There his crew feasted on coconuts, papayas, mangos, and other delicious fruits previously unknown to the Europeans.

Magellan and his crew sailed on and eventually reached the inhabited island of Limasawa. The natives were friendly and, most surprisingly, spoke the Malay language of Magellan's servant, Enrique. Magellan felt sure he was in the Moluccas, or close to them, and did not realize he had set foot for the second time in the Philippines. On a hill above Limasawa, Magellan claimed the entire archipelago for the Spanish king, Charles the First, and named it the Islands of St. Lazarus.

While on Limasawa, Magellan learned that the largest and richest island was Cebu, a few leagues away. His galleons reached Cebu on April 7, 1521. Humabon, the ruler of the island, at first tried to make Magellan pay tribute, but he was finally convinced by Enrique to become an ally of the Europeans. Humabon not only recognized Spain as the supreme ruler of his lands but also agreed to accept conversion to the Catholic faith. With great ceremony, Humabon and his followers destroyed their wooden gods, and 800 Cebuanos were baptized.

13

A Philippine stamp honoring Lapu-Lapu, the native leader who defeated the Spanish expedition led by Magellan

The peaceful conquest of Cebu looked like a great success for Magellan. Then word came that Lapu-Lapu, the chief of the neighboring small island of Mactan, refused to accept Spanish rule and to abandon his religion. Magellan decided to set an example and punish Lapu-Lapu by leading an expedition to Mactan. This was a fatal mistake.

The overconfident Magellan relied upon only 50 untrained volunteers for his fighting force. The heavy armor that his men wore made it difficult for them to move on the muddy beach of Mactan, and they were hopelessly overwhelmed by Lapu-Lapu's native army of 1,500 warriors. Magellan, who almost became the first person to sail around the world, died on April 27, 1521, fighting valiantly on the formerly unimportant Philippine island of Mactan. Chief Lapu-Lapu became a hero—the first Filipino to successfully drive out a foreign invader. An imposing statue of him now stands on Mactan.

The few survivors of Magellan's attacking force, including the historian Antonio Pigafetta, made it back to Cebu. One of Magellan's ships, captained by the Spaniard Juan Sebastian del Cano, continued the westward voyage, crossing the Indian Ocean and sailing around the southern tip of Africa. On September 6, 1522, the ship reached Seville, Spain, the starting point of Magellan's expedition three years earlier. Thus, the first voyage around the world was completed.

Four Centuries under Spain

After Magellan's expedition, the Spanish repeatedly crossed the Pacific, still seeking the fabled spices of the East. Ruy Lopez de Villalobos made one of these voyages and, in February 1543, reached the southeastern part of the island of Mindanao. Villalobos renamed some of the islands he discovered the *Felipinas*, in honor of the Spanish prince who later became King Philip II. He planned to establish a settlement in the Philippines, but his expedition failed because of lack of supplies and hostility from the natives.

Not until 1565, 44 years after Magellan's official discovery of the Philippines, did the Spanish set up a permanent settlement in the archipelago. Miguel Lopez de Legaspi, an administrator of the Spanish government in Mexico City for 30 years, was chosen by King Philip II to lead the important expedition. It sailed from Mexico on four ships carrying 400 men as well as four missionaries, who were sent to convert the Filipinos. The first Spanish colony established by Legaspi was San Miguel on Cebu Island, later called the city of Cebu. Today it is second only to the city of Manila in size.

Despite famine, mutinies, and fierce resistance by natives leaders who, like Lapu-Lapu, refused to accept Spanish

The Philippines were named after King Philip II of Spain, ruler of the powerful nation that controlled the islands for 400 years.

control, Legaspi succeeded in exploring and pacifying a large part of the archipelago. Reinforcements were sent from time to time, and by 1571, Manila, on the great bay of Luzon (now Manila Bay), was established as the capital of the Spanish colony. The spread of Islam north toward Luzon was stopped, but the Muslims were never conquered. (Even today, the Muslims, or Moros, in the south demand self-rule.) Igorots and other mountain people also resisted change.

The Spanish brought some benefits to the Philippines. They united the once-scattered and sometimes warring princedoms into a single country with a new capital. They introduced the western calendar, schools, and a common language for official business. The Spanish rulers, however, were not good administrators, and Spain's conquest of the Philippines benefited the mother country more than it did the colony.

Spanish power in the Philippines was largely in the hands of missionaries. With few Spanish troops available, many Filipino villages were controlled by missionaries, who were given plantations that were worked by the natives. The colonial government levied taxes on the crops produced by these plantations. Under this system, the missionaries dominated the population, and the schools they ran taught mainly religous subjects. Interestingly, few of the Filipino people learned to speak Spanish. It was easier for the missionaries to learn the native languages than to teach the natives Spanish.

Unfortunately for the Filipinos, the centralized government in Manila was generally wide open to corruption. The higher administrative positions were held by favorites of the king or the colonial governor rather than by qualified people. Consequently, the Filipinos were exploited both in the countryside and the cities, used purely as a source of labor for the Spanish ruling classes.

For the first 200 years of Spanish rule, the Philippines remained an unproductive colony that relied mainly on the galleon trade for support. In this trading system, Chinese merchants of silk, porcelains, diamonds, and other goods came to Manila and sold their wares to the Spanish for Mexican silver. The silver arrived on galleons from the main Spanish-Mexican port of Acapulco, and the Chinese goods were in turn loaded onto the same galleons, which then returned to Acapulco. Because of the dominance of the galleon trade, Philippine agriculture and industry—as well as the welfare of the people—were neglected.

During the late 18th century, economic conditions started to improve as tobacco, abacá (also called Manila hemp and used to make excellent rope), and sugar cane were grown and exported. More and more land was cultivated. Yet native Filipinos still held no responsible positions in Manila and

This church in the Ilocos region of Luzon was built by Spanish missionaries in the early 1700s. Its architecture combines the European baroque style with Oriental influences.

were not truly represented in the colonial government. During the first quarter of the 19th century, several revolts broke out, but they failed because of the absence of a common Filipino identity and strong leadership.

The Spanish empire itself was now experiencing a decline. It began losing its American colonies, including Mexico in 1821. During the same period, Philippine commerce increased. Newspapers were started, and a private university opened in Manila in 1859. A small, educated class of native Filipinos arose.

The Philippine Revolution

José Rizal was an early leader of the Philippine revolution.

Ironically, the seeds of the Filipino revolution were sown by these educated, well-to-do Filipinos, many of whom had studied at the university in Manila and at schools in Europe. The most prominent among them was José Rizal, who became a doctor of medicine, a poet, and a novelist. In his two novels, *Noli Me Tangere (Social Cancer)* and *El Filibusterismo (The Subversive)*, published in Europe in 1887 and 1891, he spoke out against Spanish corruption in his country. The books had to be smuggled into the Philippines, where the government considered them dangerous.

When Rizal returned to the Philippines, he and his followers established the Filipino League, dedicated to peaceful reform of the islands. Because of his political activities, Rizal was eventually arrested for treason and exiled to Dapitan, Mindanao. Unlike Rizal, other Filipinos believed that peaceful means of change were useless. They formed a secret group called *Katipunan* (a Tagalog word meaning "union"), which sought to gain reforms by force.

In 1896, fighting began. Rizal was wrongfully accused of starting the hostilities and was executed by the government. He became a martyr for the revolution. Under the leadership of Emilio Aguinaldo, the rebels continued fighting, finally forcing the Spaniards to sign the pact of Biacna-Bato. In it, the Spanish government guaranteed reforms within three years, including full civil rights for Filipinos.

But in 1898, the Spanish-American War broke out when the United States supported the independence movement of the Spanish colony of Cuba, on the other side of the world. The Philippines became immediately involved when an American squadron under Commodore George Dewey sailed to Manila from Hong Kong and destroyed the Spanish fleet in Manila Bay.

The rebel leader Aguinaldo was promised independence for the Philippines if he and his followers would help the Americans in the land battles against the Spanish. The Filipinos did their part and rejoiced when Spain was defeated in August 1898. Under the Treaty of Paris signed by Spain and the United States later that year, however, Cuba became independent, while the Philippines and other Spanish colonies such as Guam and Puerto Rico were ceded to the United States.

Aguinaldo had already declared Filipino independence and felt betrayed. American leaders claimed that while they had not entered the war to gain territory, they did not believe that the Philippines was yet ready for independence. They were perhaps influenced by the realization that controlling a country in the Orient could have military and commercial value for the United States.

Aguinaldo and his followers had no choice but to continue their struggle for independence, this time against the United States. The bloody conflict dragged on for three years until Aguinaldo was finally captured in 1901. Realizing the hopelessness of his position, he then swore an oath of allegiance to the United States.

Under the Stars and Stripes

Annexation of the Philippines was actually not popular in the United States and barely gained the final approval of the U. S. Senate. Both Democrats and Republicans, however, agreed that the American course of action must be to safeguard the welfare of the Filipino people while gradually preparing them for self-rule. Among the top priorities the government had for the Philippines were the separation of church and state and the improvement of education.

Because conditions were still unsettled, the U. S. Army briefly controlled the country, and soldiers served as the first teachers in Filipino public schools. In 1901, they were replaced by 600 civilian teachers, who arrived on an army transport ship. The Philippine Normal School was also set up to train Filipino teachers in this year.

On July 4, 1902, William Howard Taft (who would later be elected president

These soldiers were among the American troops that fought Filipino rebels following the U. S. annexation of the Philippines in 1898.

of the United States) became the first U. S. governor-general of the Philippines. To help prepare the people for democracy, the government-supported University of the Philippines was opened in Manila in 1908. Gradually, Filipinos were placed in major government jobs, and in 1916, for the first time, Filipinos elected members to their own newly created Senate and House of Representatives.

Another giant step came in 1935 when the Philippine Commonwealth was founded. Under this system, the Filipinos became self-governing and elected a president, Manuel Quezon, and vice-president, Sergio Osmeña. But the country remained a territorial possession of the United States, which retained control over its economy and its military forces. A constitution had been granted, however, and the Tydings-McDuffie Act of 1934 promised complete independence by 1946.

World War II and Independence

World War II came abruptly to the Philippines on the same day the Japanese bombed Pearl Harbor—December 7, 1941. Within a few hours, the Japanese attacked Manila, and two weeks later, they invaded the Philippines at Lingayen on Luzon.

Side by side, Filipino and American defenders fought bravely but were gradually pushed onto Luzon's Bataan Peninsula and tiny Corregidor Island. After three months of intensive Japanese bombing, Corregidor fell, and on May 6, 1942, the Philippines Commonwealth surrendered to the Japanese, who then occupied the country.

General Douglas MacArthur, who commanded the partly underground U. S. fort on Corregidor, escaped from the Philippines, along with President Quezon, two months before the surrender took place. When MacArthur left, he said the often-quoted words, "I shall return." He was flown to Australia, where he began to build a new army and an air force to recapture the Philippines. President Quezon and Vice-President Osmeña went to Washington, D. C., to establish a Commonwealth government-in-exile.

MacArthur kept his promise to return. His new army landed in the Philippines at Leyte on October 20, 1944, and, together with Filipino forces, retook the country island by island.

General Douglas MacArthur (center) returned to the Philippines on October 20, 1944, landing on the island of Leyte.

When the Japanese surrendered on September 2, 1945, the exiled Philippine government returned to Manila.

The United States kept its promise too. On July 4, 1946, the Philippines was finally granted its long-sought independence and was proclaimed the Republic of the Philippines. Manuel Roxas was elected the first president.

The Modern Philippines

Trouble for the Philippines did not end when the country gained independence. Nearly a million Filipinos died during World War II, Manila was almost totally destroyed, and the country's economy was in shambles. In addition, the government was threatened by a Communist-led group called the Huks, who made their headquarters in the mountains of central Luzon.

The Communist party had been illegal in the Philippines since 1931, but the Huks had gained strength during the war by setting themselves up as an anti-Japanese guerrilla force. During the period from 1946 to 1949, they took advantage of the weak economy and high unemployment to try and win over the people and eventually the country. Soon the Huks began to make guerrilla-style attacks against government troops.

The United States wanted to see economic and political stability in the Philippines and began giving the country both economic and military aid. Another American goal was security in the entire western Pacific. To establish a lasting presence in the area, the U. S. government signed a 99-year lease in 1947 covering the large U. S. Navy base at Subic Bay and Clark Air Base, both north of Manila.

In 1948, President Roxas died of a heart attack and was succeeded by the vice-president, Elpidio Quirino. Quirino won the presidental election in 1949 and remained in office until 1953. He was considered a corrupt leader by many, but fortunately, he had a very able and honest secretary of national defense named Ramón Magsaysay. Magsaysay reorganized the Phillipine Army and fought vigorously against the Huks. He was noted for his fair treatment of Huks and other dissidents who surrendered to the government.

Magsaysay's fairness and effectiveness against the Huks made him extremely popular, and he won the 1953 presidential election by a landslide. As president, Magsaysay established progressive policies, for example, the creation of the Presidential Complaints and Actions Committee, which speedily solved thousands of problems of ordinary Filipino citizens. He was also able to halt the Huk rebellion. Magsaysay's administration ended tragically and abruptly in 1957, however, when the president was killed in a plane crash. His less capable vice-

Ramón Magsaysay, a popular president of the Philippines, was killed in a plane crash in 1957.

calling for an end to the U. S. presence in 1991 instead of 2046.

In the 1965 presidential election, candidate Ferdinand E. Marcos stressed the urgent need for change of leadership, especially since Macapagal's land reform program had not been very effective. Marcos, a young and brilliant senator from Ilocos del Norte Province, won the election. In his first term, he had great success in boosting the country's sagging economy, and there was a period of increased prosperity. Marcos promoted the use of the newly

president, Carlos Garcia, succeeded him.

The Filipino economy slowed down under both Garcia and his successor, Diosdado Macapagal, who became president in 1961. Macapagal did begin a major land reform program, however, to abolish sharecropping. Under this system, a wealthy few owned most of the farmland, which was worked by poorly paid tenant farmers. Both leaders also took steps to make the Philippines less dependent upon the United States in economic and military matters. This rise in Filipino nationalism led to a change in the terms of the lease for the Clark and Subic Bay bases,

After serving in the House of Representatives and Senate, Ferdinand Marcos was elected president of the Philippines in 1965.

23

developed "miracle rice," a high-yield, disease-resistant strain that promised to give the Philippines its first rice surplus. He also undertook a massive public works program of building new roads, bridges, schools, health centers, and irrigation projects. In addition, Marcos began a government reform similar to that of President Magsaysay.

In the 1969 election, Ferdinand Marcos received a large vote and became the first Philippine president to win a second term. But this term did not go so smoothly. Marcos had supported the unpopular U. S. role in the Vietnam War and had even sent Filipino soldiers to fight in that conflict, although the forces were recalled soon after his reelection. Dissatisfaction with such policies led to popular demonstrations against his government.

The country also suffered another period of serious economic problems, which led to labor strikes. In agriculture, "miracle rice" did not produce extra crops as had been promised, mainly because of the lack of modern farming techniques. Adding to the general unrest was the rise of the Communist New Peoples Army (NPA), which, by the early 1970s, controlled parts of Luzon. There were also new uprisings in the south, especially on the island of Mindanao, by Muslim minorities seeking self-rule.

Marcos blamed all the unrest on the leftists or Communists and, on September 23, 1972, declared martial law in the Philippines. The Congress was dissolved, the Constitution revoked, opposition leaders were arrested, and Marcos began to rule by decree. Strict censorship of the press, radio, and television was imposed, and curfews were established. In January 1973, a new constitution was written establishing a parliamentary form of government with a National Assembly and a prime minister as well as a president. The new constituion allowed Marcos to retain absolute power and to act as both president and prime minister for an unlimited time.

During this period, Marcos began his "New Society" program, which stressed economic reform, especially better land distribution. His New Society Movement (KBL) was the Philippines' dominant political party, but the People's Power party (LABAN), led by former senator Benigno Aquino, Jr., also had a following.

In 1978, still under martial law, the Philippines held the first election for the new National Assembly, which had limited power. The KBL won the majority of the vote, and Marcos retained his title of president as well as prime minister. In January 1981, Marcos ended martial law, and in April of that year, a plebiscite, or popular election, was held that changed the form of government from a parliamentary system to one headed by a popularly elected president.

Since 1980, Benigno Aquino, Marcos' most important political opponent, had been living in self-imposed exile in

On December 14, 1985, President Marcos and his wife, Imelda, campaigned in the city of Batangas in preparation for the "snap" presidential election to be held in February 1986.

the United States. In August 1983, Aquino returned to the Philippines but was shot and killed as he was leaving the plane at the Manila airport. General Fabian Ver, chief of staff of the Philippine army, was accused of the crime, brought to trial, and acquitted. Nevertheless, Aquino's assassination and the possibility of government involvement in it seriously damaged Marcos' national and international prestige during the following years.

Under pressure from the United States to restore public confidence in the government, Marcos called for a "snap" presidential election to be held in February 1986. The opposition forces were disorganized, particularly after the death of Aquino. Eventually, however, they chose Aquino's widow, Corazon (nicknamed Cory), as their candidate. The election was monitored by U. S. and other international observers to ensure fairness. Marcos was the

Corazon Aquino opposed Ferdinand Marcos in the 1986 election.

olic Church, which supported LABAN and Corazon Aquino, thousands of Manilans took to the streets. They prevented tanks of the loyalist army forces from getting through to attack the rebels. There was some shooting, but in general, it was a remarkably peaceful revolution. Ferdinand Marcos and his wife, Imelda (who had played an important role in the government), flew from the Philippines to Hawaii, where they now live in exile. Corazon Aquino was installed as president of the Philippines in March 1986.

Yet there is still neither peace nor prosperity in the Philippines. The Communist New People's Army has grown in strength and in the violence of its attacks on the government. Economic problems persist, including very high inflation and low wages. Such problems have led to great political dissatisfaction in the Philippines. Most Filipinos consider Corazon Aquino a sincere and honest leader who wants to bring stability, democratic reform, and economic recovery to her country. Yet critics believe that, because of her lack of political experience, President Aquino moves too slowly to be an effective leader. They claim that she has not done enough to reduce the country's huge foreign debt or to provide much-needed land reform. Some critics consider her especially weak in fighting the Communist threat.

Such dissatisfaction has led to several attempts to take over the Aquino government. None of these

official winner, but it was reported that his victory was the result of massive fraud. It appeared that Corazon Aquino was the real winner, and the United States officially switched its support to her.

Soon after the election, a group of Philippine army officers, led by Vice-Chief of Staff Fidel Ramos and Defense Minister Juan Enrile, led a revolt against the Marcos government, which they considered a corrupt dictatorship. With the encouragement of the Cath-

26

After her victory in the presidential election and the subsequent revolution that ousted the Marcos government, Corazon Aquino became the leader of a country with a troubled and uncertain future.

attempts has succeeded, but the revolt led by Colonel Gregorio Honasan in August 1987 was a serious one that cost many lives. Colonel Honasan, one of the army leaders who had helped Cory Aquino overthrow Marcos, escaped with some of his followers, who are also soldiers in the Philippine Army. Honasan said that he would make another attempt to take over the government. Many believed that he wanted to set up a junta—a group of military officers who would run the country—possibly with Corazon Aquino as a "figurehead" president possessing no real power.

Three months after his escape, Honasan was arrested by military officials at a hideout near Manila. The capture of the rebel ended one of the most serious threats to the Aquino government, but other problems remained unresolved. Under the new constitution, Corazon Aquino is supposed to serve as president for one term of six years, or until 1992. With her presidency threatened by unrest and possible revolts, however, the near future of the Philippines is very uncertain.

2
EARLY IMMIGRATION TO THE UNITED STATES

During the 1500s, Spanish galleons crossed the Pacific Ocean, bringing the first Filipinos to North America.

"A Few Luzon Indians"

The profitable shipping trade between the Philippines and Mexico during the first 200 years of Spanish colonial rule was instrumental in bringing the first Filipinos to what is now the United States. The majestic Spanish galleons not only traveled between Manila and Acapulco but also explored farther. They sailed north to Japan after leaving Manila and then east toward the California coast before heading south to Acapulco.

There was always a shortage of able seamen to work on the galleons, especially because of the harsh treatment that the sailors received from the ships' captains. Indeed, many seamen "jumped" ship once they got to the shore of a new land. The Spanish captains knew that native Filipino sailors were excellent seamen and often enlisted them, sometimes by force, for service on the galleons. In

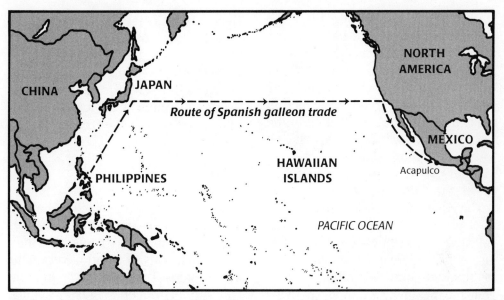

During the 17th century, Spanish galleons traveled between the Philippines and Mexico, trading the silks and gems of Asia for silver from the New World. On their way to the Mexican port of Acapulco, the ships often stopped on the California coast.

fact, the galleon *San Pablo*, which began the Acapulco-Manila trade in 1565, included Filipinos in its crew. Four Filipinos were among those who died before the ship reached Santa Barbara Channel Island, off the California coast, after a particularly rough trip.

Other Filipino sailors, called "a few Luzon Indians" by the Spaniards, were slightly more fortunate. They sailed on the *Nuestra Señora de Esperanza (Our Lady of Hope),* commanded by Pedro de Unamuno, which took a similar route to California in 1587. On October 18 of that year, the ship entered Morro Bay (near present-day San Luis Obispo, California) and sent a landing party to shore. The party included the "Luzon Indians," who served as scouts and carried swords as protection against the native California Indians.

The landing party took official possession of the area for Spain by putting up a cross made of branches. The group was attacked by native American Indians, however, and one of the Filipinos was killed. Heavy fog rolled in, and Unamuno and his crew gave up further exploration of that part of the California coast.

Other Spanish captains were more successful. Sebastian Vizcaino, for example, charted the coast in 1596 and founded Monterey as a repair station for ships coming from the Philippines. By the late 18th century, there was a line of Spanish settlements from San Francisco to San Diego. Undoubtedly, many of the thousands of Filipinos who served as seamen in the galleon trade chose to stay in the New World. Antonio Miranda, believed to be a Filipino, was one of the 46 founders of the settlement of Los Angeles in 1781.

The Spanish galleons also sailed to New Orleans. It is on record that "Manilamen," as they were often called, jumped ship there in 1763, thus becoming the first confirmed Filipino immigrants to the United States and perhaps the first Asian immigrants as well. These same immigrants made New Orleans the oldest Filipino settlement.

In order to escape capture by the Spanish, Manilamen fled to Louisiana's remote bayous and marshes. The offspring of those pioneers founded the Filipino settlements of St. Malo, Bernard Parish; Leon Rojas at Bayou Cholas; Bassa Bassa, Jefferson Parish; and the Alambro Canal.

The original Manilamen became fishermen and introduced the technique of sun-drying Louisiana shrimp so that they could be exported. They intermarried with earlier Spanish and French immigrants to Louisiana, and their descendants are sometimes called "Filipino Creoles." During the 1800s, the Filipino communities prospered, and on July 24, 1870, they founded the Spanish-speaking Hispano-Filipino Benevolent Society of New Orleans, perhaps the first Filipino social club in the United States. By the 1900s, there were over 2,000 people of Filipino ancestry in the New Orleans area alone. A Filipino center was located on Dumaine Street, near the French Market.

Pensionados

The first Filipinos officially admitted into the United States were *pensionados*—students who came to study under pensions or small government scholarships. The *pensionado* program was authorized on August 26, 1903, and began two months later when about 100 promising young Filipinos arrived in California. By 1905, *Filipino Students Magazine* was being published in Berkeley, California, and by 1912 some 209 Filipino men and women had earned degrees or advanced their education in about 50 U. S. colleges and universities. Generally, *pensionados* were well-treated in the United States because they were members of a small group with high educational goals and were considered "short-term immigrants."

The *pensionado* program was designed to help prepare Filipinos for self-government. It was intended that the *pensionados* would return to the Philippines after graduation. The majority did return and became leaders in their specialties, but others stayed and pursued opportunities in the

Young Filipinos studying in the United States formed many social and educational clubs. This photograph from 1927 features the Philippinesians of George Washington University in Washington, D.C.

United States. Those who returned, according to one historian, "proved to be zealous exponents of democracy and the American way of life." They persuaded other Filipinos to come to the United States for their education. Whether they returned to the Philippines or remained in the United States, *pensionados* rendered valuable services to both countries in science, engineering, education, law, and other fields.

The *pensionado* system was temporarily suspended when World War I broke out in 1914, then revived in 1919 after a truce was declared. By the 1920s, the official *pensionados* were joined by an increasing number of Filipinos who came to the United States to study but who were either on partial pensions or without pensions. The latter called themselves "self-supporting students" and eventually outnumbered the *pensionados*.

Most of the self-supporting students were young, single males who first settled in college towns in the Midwest and the East. Chicago, with its outstanding schools, became the site of one of the earliest and largest concentrations of Filipinos. This was the start of the so-called "Little Manilas" in various cities.

As early as the 1920s, Filipinos could be found in an amazing variety of U. S. locations, where they invariably set up Filipino social or educational clubs. In 1922, for example, Filipino students at George Washington University in Washington, D.C., formed the Philippensians. Similar groups sprang up in Minnesota (Filipinosotans, founded in 1925); Des Moines, Iowa; Kansas City, Kansas (Kansas City Filipinos); Moscow, Idaho (Filipino Idahoans); Ithaca, New York (Philippine Collegians); Jonesboro, Arkansas; Angola, Indiana; Vernonia, Oregon (Filipino Brotherhood, founded 1929); Lincoln, Nebraska; Butte, Montana; and in the big cities of the East. There were also students in Hawaii.

The self-supporting students were both flexible and versatile, taking whatever jobs they could to support

Members of the Young Philippines Future Fliers Association of Maui, Hawaii, pose in front of their airplane in 1936.

themselves while going to school. Most were unskilled and, as members of a minority group, were excluded from many fields. They worked as hotel doormen, bellboys, busboys, kitchen helpers, domestic servants, waiters, cooks, housepainters, and laborers of all kinds. In 1924, more than a hundred students obtained nighttime jobs in the Chicago Post Office as letter sorters. One of them, José Dumpit, founded and became the first president of the Filipino Postal Club of Chicago.

Another self-supporting student was Pedro M. Blanco, whose father was a captain in the Kaptipunan forces that had fought against Spain and the United States. Blanco landed in California in 1917 with $3.50 in his pocket. He got a job picking fruit and worked his way through both high school and his freshman year at the University of California. Later, he worked in the wheat fields of Kansas and earned enough money for a ticket to New York, where he entered Columbia University in 1922. During the summers, Blanco went from city to city selling Filipino hats and embroideries. He also made money for his education by giving lectures on the need for Philippine independence. Because he was such an effective orator, Blanco was invited to speak on the topic of Philippine independence in opposition to the former governor of Massachusetts. After several years of hard work, Pedro Blanco finally received a degree from the Columbia School of Business in 1924.

A typical early Filipino-American magazine, *The Republic*, published in Washington, D.C., from 1924 to 1933, included similar student success stories on a special page titled "Making Good in the U. S." By the late 1930s, there had been more than 500 *pensionados* and about 14,000 self-supporting students who had come to the United States. The economic hardship of the depression, however, caused a sharp decline in Filipino enrollment.

Sakadas

By far, the first sizable Filipino immigration occurred in Hawaii from 1906 to about 1934. This is sometimes called the "first wave" of Filipino immigrants, even though they were preceded by the small but dynamic groups of Filipino students.

There had been a few Filipinos who had come to Hawaii prior to 1906. Perhaps some arrived on Spanish galleons crossing the Pacific. During the 19th century, Manilamen also served on whaling ships that docked at Honolulu during winter.

It was during the 19th century, too, that Hawaii began to develop its sugar and pineapple industries. By 1900, five huge American companies dominated the industries and owned plantations requiring thousands of men to work them. The Big Five, as the companies were called, hired their field workers through the Hawaiian Sugar Planters'

Japanese laborers like this woman loading sugar cane were among the many Asian immigrants who worked on the plantations of Hawaii.

Association (HSPA). Chinese laborers did the very tiring work until 1882, when a law was passed that prevented Chinese immigration to the United States. Hawaii would not become a U. S. territory until 1900, but since the planters hoped that the islands would be annexed, they stopped importing Chinese laborers. Koreans and Japanese took their places, but labor strikes and other problems eventually caused the plantation owners to look for a new source of laborers.

In 1906, Albert F. Judd, a lawyer for the Big Five and later chief justice of the Hawaii Supreme Court, spent six months in the Philippines trying to recruit Filipino workers. He could find only 15 volunteers. On the afternoon of December 20, 1906, the ship *Doric* landed in Honolulu with the recruits, ranging in age from 14 to 56. They were all from the Ilocos region of northern Luzon, which was heavily populated but agriculturally barren. Besides being energetic and thrifty, the Ilocanos had a reputation for being willing travelers, but only about 100 more of them came to Hawaii in 1907. The main reason for the small number was that the HSPA would not pay for the return of the men after they had completed their three-year contract. These laborers called themselves *Sakadas*, which means "contract workers" in Tagalog.

No recruiting was done in 1908, but in 1909, the HSPA tried new tactics, and large-scale recruiting got under-

Filipinos working on a pineapple plantation in Hawaii during the 1930s

way. Filipino agents were hired as recruiters and were given 10 to 15 pesos (five to seven dollars) for each person they recruited. Starting in 1915, the HSPA paid the *Sakadas'* return fares and provided housing for them. The recruiters also went from town to town showing free, specially made movies that pictured the positive side to life in Hawaii. This recruiting campaign was highly successful.

In 1924, the United States government passed an immigration act that excluded the entry of Chinese, Japanese, and other Oriental peoples but increased quotas for Filipinos. This further encouraged immigration from the Philippines. From 1906 to 1934, about 120,000—mostly single men from the Ilocos region—came to Hawaii and chose to stay, many going on to the mainland. In 1934, however, the Tydings-McDuffie Act promising independence to the Philippines suddenly limited entries to the United States to only 50 a year.

For the impressive numbers of Filipino immigrants who came to Hawaii, plantation life was hardly ideal. Work in the fields, which included hoeing, weeding, cutting, loading, and hauling, started before sunup and lasted eight or nine hours. It was backbreaking labor, the pay was low, and housing conditions were miserable.

Pablo Manlapit, a *Sakada* who came to Hawaii in 1910, was so disturbed by the conditions faced by his countrymen that he set out to help them. Like other *Sakadas,* Manlapit worked as a field hand, but he was promoted quickly to foreman and then to time-keeper. He was soon fired from the plantation, however, because he led strikes. Manlapit moved to the city of Hilo and, in 1913-1914, organized the Filipino Unemployment Association.

After leaving the plantation, Manlapit held jobs as an interpreter, a newspaper editor, a stevedore, and a janitor in a law office, but he still had time to study. In 1919, he became the first Filipino in Hawaii to pass the law examinations. That same year, he started the Filipino Labor Union (also called Filipino Federation of Labor). In 1920, with the help of Japanese labor officials, he helped launch a Hawaii-wide strike for better wages and working conditions, but it was broken by strikebreakers and an influenza epidemic.

Throughout his life, Pablo Manlapit continued to fight for better working conditions in Hawaii. There were many

Pablo Manlapit led the effort to improve working conditions for Filipino immigrants in Hawaii during the early 1900s.

strikes, and life was difficult for plantation workers. It was only in the late 1930s that the unions finally gained pay increases and other improvements. In 1950, the power of the Big Five was finally broken, along with the old plantation system that had exploited so many Filipinos and others. Also by the 1950s, many Filipinos had started their own businesses or entered the professions and had become respected middle-class citizens of Hawaii. In 1959, they also became full-fledged citizens of the United States, when Hawaii became the 50th state in the union.

California Days

California and Washington also lured thousands of Filipinos after the passage of the new immigration law in 1924. The Immigration Act of 1924 set up strict yearly quotas for most immigrant groups and completely excluded the majority of Orientals. Chinese, Japanese, Koreans, and most other Oriental people were not allowed to immigrate to the United States. Filipinos were exempt from these restrictions, however, because they were American "nationals." They traveled with U. S. passports, although they were not citizens because the Philippines was an American territory, not a state. Legally they could not be excluded.

With the passage of the 1924 Act, California farmers and cannery operators in the Pacific Northwest and Alaska were suddenly deprived of cheap Oriental labor. They were forced to accept Filipino workers as well as Mexicans, who were exempt from the quotas established by the immigration law. Soon, about 4,000 to 5,000 Filipino laborers were arriving each year in West Coast cities like Los Angeles, San Francisco, and Seattle.

Like the *Sakadas* of Hawaii, the West Coast immigrants were almost all young, single men who wanted to improve their lives or who were seeking adventure and travel. They called themselves "Pinoys" (from the masculine ending of the Spanish word "Filipino"), and like the *Sakadas,* they found that immigrant life was not as bright as had been promised.

Agriculture was California's biggest industry, and it required 10-hour days of "stoop labor," which meant stooping down to pick or cut fields full of lettuce, asparagus, cauliflower, peas, celery, beets, tomatoes, or spinach. Most of the Filipinos worked on large farms in the fertile San Joaquin, Salinas, Sacramento, and Imperial valleys. Stockton, an inland port in the San Joaquin Valley, became their agricultural headquarters.

In Oregon and Washington, Pinoys harvested hops and orchard fruits around Salem and in the Yakima Valley. The lumber industry of these states also attracted Pinoys. Around Puget Sound in Washington, thousands of Filipinos worked in the salmon canneries, especially during the 1930s.

No matter where they worked, Pinoys were paid low wages for very hard labor and usually lived in shacks, tents, or below-standard rooms. Carlos Bulosan, who came to Seattle in 1931 as a field worker and later became a best-selling author, said Filipinos were the lowest-paid workers in the United States. Far worse than the low wages, though, were the prejudice and violence that they faced.

During this same period, there were few race problems for Filipino immigrants in Hawaii because the population of the islands was made up of so many different racial groups. By contrast, the same bitter prejudice that excluded the Japanese and other

Orientals by the Immigration Act of 1924 also struck the new Filipino immigrants in California. "Positively No Filipinos Allowed" and "No Filipinos Wanted" signs were common.

Filipinos in California were discriminated against because they were looked upon as members of an inferior race. They were paid less than other workers doing the same jobs and were prevented from renting rooms in good neighborhoods. As a result, Filipinos were often forced into overcrowded conditions, like the 60 Pinoys in the San Joaquin Valley who lived in a barn, 20 sleeping in the loft and 40 on the barn floor. Filipinos were also denied service in restaurants, movie houses, swimming pools, barbershops, and bowling alleys.

Legal restrictions were used to limit the rights of the Filipinos in California. They were prohibited by law from marrying whites. (Similar laws were enacted in Idaho, Nevada, and Oregon.) California and other western states also made it difficult for the professionals among the Filipinos to get licenses as doctors, teachers, lawyers, engineers, and nurses. This caused many professionals to move to the Midwest or the East.

Faced with this kind of discrimination, most Filipinos remained calm, polite, and hardworking. They were puzzled to learn, however, that Americans preached democracy but did not always practice it.

In 1928, California Congressman Richard J. Welch introduced a law in the U. S. House of Representatives that excluded further Filipino immigrants, but the law did not pass. The tide of immigrants was difficult to stop because the California farmers and the Hawaiian sugar and pineapple growers needed laborers.

During this period, the Filipinos came to realize that laws and institutions could work in their favor as well as against them. They began to form agricultural unions to protect their liberties and their rights to fair wages. The Filipino agricultural union movement started in 1930, and strikes and violence soon followed. Vigilante groups were formed, and a wave of race riots erupted. Writer Carlos Bulosan was the victim of several beatings that put him in the Los Angeles County Hospital for two years. "I feel like a criminal...," he wrote, "and the crime is that I am a Filipino American."

Despite the attacks made on them, thousands of Filipinos united to form the Filipino Labor Union (FLU) in December 1933. The FLU worked toward several goals: a minimum wage of 35 cents an hour, an eight-hour day, employment without regard to race, and acceptance of the union as a hiring and bargaining agent. The economic depression of the early 1930s, however, made achieving these goals difficult. Finally, some 7,000 Filipinos joined with white and Mexican workers to strike and paralyze the California lettuce

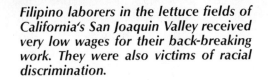

Filipino laborers in the lettuce fields of California's San Joaquin Valley received very low wages for their back-breaking work. They were also victims of racial discrimination.

industry in 1934. The lettuce farmers met some of the workers' demands, but significant progress was not made until the Filipino Agricultural Laborers Association was formed in 1938.

By 1940, this multiracial organization had 30,000 members in California alone. Carlos Bulosan observed that, with the formation of the Agricultural Laborers Association, the social awakening of the Filipinos was finally taking shape.

Alaskeros

Alaska was the third largest Filipino population center in the United States after Hawaii and California. The numbers of Filipinos in Alaska varied widely, however, because of the seasonal nature of the work in the salmon canneries where they were employed.

The first Filipinos in Alaska probably came as crewmen aboard whaling ships that cruised the Bering Sea and the Arctic Ocean during the 19th century. Then in 1909, the Alaska canneries hired recruiters to persuade several hundred Filipinos living in California to come to Alaska. Some of the recruits stayed—the 1910 census shows there were 246 Filipinos living in the territory. By the 1920s, many more were arriving. They were mostly self-supporting students, there to earn money in the spring and summer when they were not attending school. Others were migrant workers who traveled up from the farms in California and Washington.

Carlos Bulosan was a field worker in California during the violent years of the 1920s and 1930s. He later became a successful writer.

In 1937, these Filipino immigrants worked at the Wrangell Cannery in Alaska, processing and packing salmon.

Money was supposed to be easy to make in Alaska, but the pay was actually not much—$45 a month, or $300 for a six-month season. The cannery workers, who called themselves "Alaskeros," worked from 6:00 A.M. to 6:00 P.M., hauling the salmon in from boats and onto trucks that took the fish to the canneries. Wearing rubber aprons and boots, the Alaskeros then hosed down the fish, sorted them out with hooks, cut off their heads and tails, cleaned them out, and cooked, canned, and sealed them. Other jobs included making wooden boxes and packing the cans for shipment south.

Because Alaska's population included native Alaskans (Eskimos) and other Asian workers, Filipinos faced less prejudice there than in California. Nevertheless, injustices did occur in the big salmon canneries, and by 1936, the Alaskeros had formed their first cannery workers' union.

Some of the Filipino cannery workers married Eskimos, and soon there was an established community to give stability to the lives of the immigrants. A social club, the Filipino Community of Juneau, was formed in 1935 and still exists today. In 1930, there were 4,200 Alaskeros working in the canneries. By 1940, the number had grown to about 9,000. During that same year, the total Filipino population of the United States was estimated at 128,000, including 53,000 in the territory of Hawaii.

Filipino Sailors

Beginning before World War I, adventurous young Filipinos found that the easiest way to see the world and especially the United States was to enlist in the U. S. Navy. They signed up in recruiting offices at the American naval base at Cavite, across the bay from Manila. As U. S. nationals, Filipinos were eligible to enlist, but there was one catch: they were usually limited to positions as stewards. This classification included cooks, waiters, pantrymen, dishwashers, custodians, and valets (servants) for admirals and other officers.

This situation continued through World War II, but it did not deter the majority of Filipinos who joined the service. The pay and the living condi-

tions were good and the men got to travel, but the most positive aspect was that those who served in the navy or the marines for three years were eligible for U.S. citizenship. Many went beyond this limit and made 20-year careers out of the navy, retiring with benefits.

Despite the restrictions, not all Filipinos in the navy remained stewards. Some advanced because of their own special abilities. For example, in 1925, Leon Morales of the USS *California* was praised by his superior officer as "exceptionally capable, accurate and honest in the handling of the ship's books and daily funds." Others took educational courses, even while at sea.

By the 1920s, there were about 4,000 Filipinos in the navy, mostly travel-minded Ilocanos. When they retired, many settled in navy towns like San Diego, California, or Norfolk, Virginia. As citizens they were able to purchase property, contributing further to developing Filipino-American communities.

Filipinos who enlisted in the U.S. Merchant Marine were not as lucky as their countrymen in the navy. Excellent sailors like all Filipinos, they were much in demand, and as many as 7,870 had joined the merchant marine by 1930. But the Merchant Marine Act passed in 1936 required that 75 percent of crews aboard American cargo, passenger, and fishing vessels be U. S. citizens. This immediately left up to 5,000 Filipino seamen

These colorful sailboats, known as vintas, are part of the long Filipino tradition of seafaring. In the 1920s and 1930s, Filipino sailors put their skills to use on board ships in the U. S. Navy and Merchant Marine.

unemployed, some of whom had 10 to 15 years of honorable service. The loss of the experienced Filipino sailors particularly affected the Filipino populations in the ports of Baltimore, New Orleans, and New York.

American-born sailors played a role in the growth of Filipino-American communities by marrying Filipino women while they were stationed in the Philippines. The wives and children of these marriages became American citizens and eventually came to make their homes in the United States.

3
THE TURNING POINT:
WORLD WAR II TO THE THIRD WAVE

A steward in the U. S. Navy poses with a poster portraying the fighting spirit of the Filipino people.

Fighting Side by Side

Another way for Filipinos to come to the United States was to enlist in the U.S. Army at posts in the Philippines, although there was no guarantee that these men would be assigned to the States. There were some 25,000 Filipinos who volunteered for duty in the U. S. forces (army and navy) during World War I, most because of a genuine desire to fight for democracy.

Ironically, Filipinos who fought for the United States' causes were unable to enjoy the benefits of democracy as American citizens did. The Americanization process in the Philippines had given them a strong respect for democratic government, however, and they hoped one day to secure it for their own country. Many thousands died fighting for the democratic ideal. The first Filipino in the U. S. Army to give his life in World War I was Private Thomas Claudio, who died fighting in Europe.

Members of the First Filipino Regiment training in California, 1943

On December 7, 1941, when the Japanese attacked Pearl Harbor and Manila, thousands of Filipino-Americans felt an intense patriotic call to help both the country of their birth (or parents' birth), the Philippines, and their new home, the United States. In California alone, some 16,000 Filipinos registered for the first draft. There were 80,000 who did so throughout the continental United States and in Hawaii. The problem was that under the Selective Service Act of 1940, only U. S. citizens were eligible to serve in the armed forces. Most Filipinos living in United States were nationals—neither citizens nor aliens. Because of their status, they were also not permitted to work in defense factories.

To overcome these injustices, prominent Filipinos in the United States wrote letters to the secretary of war and to President Franklin D. Roosevelt. The letters worked. On December 20, 1941, President Roosevelt issued a proclamation amending the Selective Service Act and giving Filipinos the right both to serve in the armed forces and to work in defense factories.

In April 1942, the First Filipino Infantry Battalion was formed at Camp San Luis Obispo, California. It was under the command of Lieutenant Colonel Robert H. Offley, an American who spoke fluent Tagalog because he had spent his youth on Mindoro, where his father was governor. Under his command were Filipino officers and men. The battalion was so large, however, that it was reorganized on July 13, 1942, into the First Filipino Regiment and Band. This larger group had 143 officers, 6 warrant officers, and 3,019 men, all Filipinos. Later, on November 21, 1942, the Second Filipino Infantry Regiment was formed at Camp Cooke, California.

The men of the two Filipino regiments were trained for jungle warfare so they could lead the way in recapturing the Philippines from the Japanese. Many were already familiar with the terrain but were given special instruction in intelligence (gathering military information), the Japanese language, radio communications, judo, mapmaking, demolition, booby traps, and survival. At different times during the war, the regiments were sent to Australia, the Philippines, and New Guinea. Prior to going overseas, 1,200 of the men stood proudly in a V formation on the Camp Beale parade ground in California on February 20, 1943. In a radio-broadcast ceremony, they became U. S. citizens. Another mass naturalization took place later in the Santa Barbara City Hall. Similar ceremonies were repeated wherever Filipino-Americans served.

In 1943, these Filipino-American sailors took the oath of citizenship at a base in Iceland where they were stationed.

A select group of men drawn from the regiments formed the First Reconnaissance Battalion (Special), a commando unit. During the campaign to retake the Philippines, the commandos parachuted or went by submarine into key areas. They disguised themselves as village traders or other local people but were secretly gathering information about the Japanese installations and troop movements. This information was radioed back to other U. S. troops near the area or to Australia at a rate of nearly 4,000 messages a month. The commandos also destroyed Japanese communications lines.

Other Filipino-American soldiers were called "Coast Watchers"—they radioed important information on enemy ship movements and weather conditions that affected military operations. This work was often dangerous since the watchers were sometimes under enemy fire. Members of the First and Second regiments also served in the joint parachute-naval assault to recapture Corregidor in 1944.

Thanks to the often-heroic deeds of the Filipino-American volunteers, the Philippines was finally liberated. Many of these gallant men earned the Bronze Star and other medals. Among them were Californians Staff Sergeant Paulino A. Rosales, Stockton; Corporal Ralph M. Balunes, Los Angeles; and Technician Teodore M. Taluban, Salinas.

In addition to the Filipino troops on land, about 15,000 Filipinos served above and beneath the sea, in submarines and on ships, not only as stewards but also as seamen, engineers, radio operators, firemen, and deckhands. Pinoys also volunteered for the marines and the coast guard. An uncounted number of Filipinos served in the Army Air Corps in jobs from clerks to airplane mechanics.

At home in the United States, Filipinos loyally guarded their country as members of Filipino units in the California State Militia. Others, including Filipinas (women from the Philippines), worked in California and Washington aircraft factories or raised money for bonds for the war effort.

After the War

Filipino-Americans had dramatically proven their loyalty to the United States, despite years of discrimination and violence. Americans finally recognized this devotion to democratic ideals and the tremendous contributions the Filipinos had made.

As a result, there was a positive change of attitude toward Filipinos. Many fighting men had already been made citizens. In 1941 and 1943 respectively, Washington state and California gave Filipino nationals the legal right to own property (previously they were barred from ownership). And on July 2, 1946, two days before the Philippines achieved independence, President Harry S. Truman signed the Filipino Naturalization Act, which gave resident

Filipinos the right to become citizens. The law opened up new possibilities for Filipinos to seek equality in areas previously closed to them. In 1948, the California Supreme Court ruled that laws forbidding interracial marriages were unconstitutional.

The passage of the War Brides Act in 1946 also affected Filipino-Americans. This act allowed resident Filipinos who had served in the U. S. Armed Forces in the Philippines and who had married there to bring their wives, children, and other dependents to the United States. The same law permitted the immigration of former Philippine Scouts (soldiers who served under U. S. officers in the Philippines during the territorial period), along with their wives and children. As a result of this legislation, California's Filipino population more than doubled between 1940 and 1960, going from about 31,000 to about 65,000.

The influx of immigrants between 1950 and 1960 is usually considered the second wave of Filipino immigration. As the Filipino population in the United States increased, new employment opportunities opened up in areas such as the aircraft, electronics, and chemical industries. In contrast to the first-wave Filipinos, who were largely agricultural laborers restricted from other employment, the newer immigrants were able to find jobs as clerks and accountants, and in many other fields formerly closed to them. The civil rights laws passed in 1948 helped lift racial barriers in government jobs, attracting Filipinos and also encouraging private businesses to hire them.

Another major turning point for Filipinos and other minorities also occurred in 1948 when President Truman abolished discrimination in the U. S. Armed Forces. As a result of this measure, Filipinos in the navy were no longer restricted to being stewards. By the mid-1980s, there were about 400 officers of Filipino ancestry in the U. S. Navy.

Back in the Philippines, one interesting aftereffect of World War II was that thousands of U. S. army jeeps were repainted and turned into "jeepneys," or taxis. Today these colorful and reliable vehicles are a symbol of the Philippines. They may be seen as a symbol, too, of the versatility and energy of the Filipino people, both in the Philippines and the United States.

The Third Wave

After World War II, large numbers of Filipinos came to California under the provisions of the War Brides Act and other special legislation. A new immigration law, however, signed on July 4, 1946, the date of Philippine independence, limited the national quota of Filipino immigrants to 100 per year. The quota was a hardship on Filipinos who wanted to immigrate but who were not covered by the War Brides Act.

After World War II, the colorful taxis called jeepneys became symbols of the Philippines and its resourceful people.

In 1965, at the foot of the Statue of Liberty, President Lyndon B. Johnson signed a new immigration law abolishing the old system, which was based on varying quotas for individual countries. Instead, a yearly world quota of immigrants was set at 290,000, with no individual country allowed to send more than 20,000 immigrants in one year. The increase in Filipino immigrants was immediate. Between 1961 and 1985, nearly 683,000 Filipinos came to make new homes in the United States. These newcomers made up the third wave of Filipino immigration.

The new law favored the entry of relatives of people already in the United States and of professionals such as doctors, lawyers, engineers, nurses, pharmacists, scientists, and people in technical fields. Filipinos in these professions, both men and women, came to the United States. They came for a variety of reasons—to increase their technical skills, to study on scholarships, to join their families, to get married, and for political or financial reasons.

Today, Filipinos are the fastest-growing Asian minority in the United States. There are now more than 800,000 Filipinos in the country, with that number estimated to rise to a million by 1990. In the continental United States, the largest Filipino populations are in these cities: San Francisco-Oakland; Los Angeles; Chicago; San Diego; New York; Seattle; Stockton and San Jose, California; and Norfolk, Virginia.

All these communities have Filipino newspapers, and newspapers often reflect how people live and think. Invariably, the most popular stories reported in the Filipino papers are those of high educational accomplishments by children. Hard work and attention to study, Filipinos believe, are the only sure paths to success, especially in the United States.

49

4
CONTRIBUTIONS TO AMERICAN LIFE

Dancer, choreographer, and writer, Reynaldo Alejandro is one of many talented Filipino-Americans.

The Arts

Artists were among the earliest Filipino immigrants to the United States, and they have since contributed to almost every area of American art.

Illustrator Manuel Ray Isip came to the United States in 1925 to further his art studies. From 1926 to 1928, he was one of the best illustrators for the *New York American* newspaper. Later, he was a layout artist and designer at Columbia Pictures and 20th Century-Fox for many years. Isip also founded the Associated Philippine Artists and arranged exhibits of his paintings and those of other Filipino artists in the United States. His son, Manuel Ray Isip, Jr., had a distinguished career in industrial art and was one of the top automobile designers for Ford and Chrysler.

Mario Yrissary, whose grandfather was half Apache Indian and half Irish and whose grandmother was a Filipina, came to the United States in 1945 at the age of 12. He studied at the Cooper Union School of Fine Arts in New York and eventually became one of the foremost American abstract painters, specializing in intricate and colorful grid patterns. Yrissary's paintings are included in major modern art collections. Two of his works, *Spine* and *Throb*, are in the Joseph H. Hirshhorn Museum, part of the Smithsonian Institution in Washington, D.C.

Val M. Laigo, for 20 years an assistant professor of art at Seattle University, began his career as an artist in 1951 and has worked in many mediums and styles. His three-paneled abstract mural, *East Is West*, which is on display in Seattle's José Rizal Park, is made of mosaic tiles, glass, and mirrors set in concrete and steel. The work symbolizes the blending of the Filipino and American cultures. A large mural portraying human creativity is in the Reading Room of Seattle University's A. A. Lemieux Library, while another major work is displayed in the Boeing

Val M. Laigo displays three of his impressive abstract paintings.

José Aruego

Scientific Research Laboratories, also in Seattle. Laigo's works have been exhibited in Los Angeles, New York, and Mexico City and have won many awards.

José Aruego is widely acclaimed as one of the best American graphic artists and illustrators of children's books. He started out as a lawyer in his native Manila but began to draw cartoons for the *Saturday Evening Post*, *Look*, and other magazines when he came to the United States in the 1960s. His first children's book was *The King and His Friends* in 1969. Since then, he

has illustrated more than three dozen books for young readers, among them *Juan and the Asuangs, Leo the Late Bloomer,* and *Where Are You Going, Little Mouse?* The books have been translated into Japanese, German, French, Spanish, Swedish, and Dutch, but not Tagalog. In 1977, Aruego was named "Outstanding Filipino Overseas," an honor bestowed by the Philippine Department of Tourism and the Philippine Jaycees.

In Hawaii, Francisco "Corky" Trinidad is a well-known editorial cartoonist. Named after a character in the comic strip "Gasoline Alley," Corky has been with the *Honolulu Star Bulletin* since 1969. His cartoons have also appeared in 20 other newspapers and magazines, including the *Los Angeles Times*, the Paris *Herald Tribune, Time*, and *Newsweek*.

Filipino-Americans are among the leading comic-book artists in the United States. Alfred Alcala draws the character "Voltar," while Rudy Nebres specializes in kung fu themes for Marvel Comics. Edna Jundis is with Women's Comix, and Frank Magsimo draws comic-book covers.

Among other distinguished Filipino-American artists are Orlando S. Lagman, portrait painter of presidents; watercolorist Venancio C. Igarta; photographer Inocencio Padua; film animator and magazine art director Edgardo B. Soller; fashion designer Ruben Panis; and landscape painter A. Sabater.

Music

Music is in the heart of every Filipino and Filipina. Even before the first *Sakadas* arrived in Hawaii in 1906, three Filipinos were members of the Royal Hawaiian Band. There have been countless Filipino-American musical talents since then.

In the world of opera, Evelyn Mandac has been internationally acclaimed. She came to the United States in 1964 on a Fulbright scholarship and received a master's degree from the Juilliard School in New York City. Mandac made both her professional debut and her Metropolitan Opera debut in 1968. Among the classic operas in which she performed were *La Bohéme, Carmen, The Marriage of Figaro,* and *The Magic Flute.* She also sang with many major U. S. orchestras, including the Chicago Symphony and the Philadelphia Orchestra, and performed in Canada and Europe. Her varied career included television appearances and recordings for RCA and Seraphim. Evelyn Mandac retired in 1986, but her talent will not soon be forgotten.

Filipino-American singers have also performed on Broadway. Cely Carillo Onrubia came to the United States on a scholarship and studied at Juilliard. Upon graduation in 1960, she became the understudy to Miyoshi Umeki, who had a leading role in the musical *Flower Drum Song.* A year later, she took over the role and became the first Filipina star on Broadway. After a 5-

Evelyn Mandac

month run of the musical on Broadway and an 18-month national tour, Cely left the stage to appear in TV programs and films. During Liberty Weekend in 1986, she sang the "Star-Spangled Banner" for the unveiling of the newly restored Statue of Liberty.

Cely Onrubia's daughter, Cynthia, made her own Broadway debut in 1977 as a dancer-singer in *A Chorus Line.* Cynthia, who began her career as a child doing commercials for Lux soap on television, finished a 14-month Broadway engagement in the musical *Songs and Dances* late in 1986.

One of the most respected Filipino-American musicians is classical guitarist Michael Dadap. Dadap was the leader of a rock and roll band while studying at the University of Manila, but he was always drawn to classical music. He came to the United States in 1971 to study guitar at the Juilliard School and the Mannes College of Music in New York. Dadap now performs 40 concerts per year and teaches music at several colleges, in addition to composing and making records. He is also president of the nonprofit Children's Orchestra Society, Inc., of New York, which features about 50 mostly Asian-American kids four to seven years old. The group has performed in the United States, including concerts at Carnegie Hall, as well as overseas.

Classical guitarist Michael Dadap (above) also serves as director of a group of talented young musicians (right).

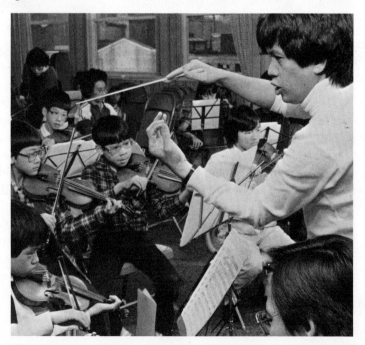

Members of the Philippine Dance Company perform a traditional Filipino dance.

Dance

The Tinikling is a favorite Philippine dance in which the performers dance around and between two bamboo poles clapped rhythmically together on the floor. This is only one of the many colorful dances performed by Philippine dance groups throughout the United States. Probably the oldest of these groups is the Philippine Dance Company of New York, founded in 1943 by Bruna P. Seril. In 1969, the multi-talented Reynaldo G. Alejandro became its artistic director and choreographer.

Reynaldo, or "Ronnie," began dancing at age 15 after studying books about American dancer Martha Graham. He joined the Filipinescas Dance Company in the Philippines and, with the group, toured Europe, the Middle East, North and Central America, and China. Upon his return to the Philippines, he continued dancing professionally and also attended school, receiving a master's degree in library science.

In 1969, Reynaldo Alejandro came to New York to study dance at the Martha Graham School. He also got a job as the reference librarian of the New

The versatile Reynaldo Alejandro has written several books about Filipino cooking and works as a chef in his own catering company.

joined the Joffrey Ballet, then the Grands Ballets Canadiens in Montreal, and finally the Atlanta Ballet. Barredo has danced all the great female roles in classical ballet, including those in *Swan Lake, The Nutcracker, Sleeping Beauty,* and *Romeo and Juliet.*

Since the early 1960s, Seattle's colorful Cumbanchero Percussioners, Mandayan Marchers, and Princessas have achieved their own fame as performers. They are the nation's only Filipino-American marching units and have thrilled thousands of parade spectators and TV viewers with their appearances. These marching groups are made up of young people who wear native costumes, chant native dialects, and play an assortment of Filipino and American instruments.

York Public Library's dance collection. In addition to these activities, Ronnie founded the Reynaldo Alejandro Dance Theatre, Inc., wrote extensively on dance in the *New York Times* and other publications, and authored a book entitled *Philippine Dance.*

Maniya Barredo has been the prima ballerina of the Atlanta Ballet for 10 years. She came to the United States in 1970 to study with the American Ballet Center. Two years later, she

Maniya Barredo

Members of the Cumbanchero marching units on parade

Movies and Television

Filipinos have been in American films since silent-movie days. Because of their exotic-looking faces and their ready availability to the California movie industry, they were used in crowd scenes in such early classics as *The Thief of Baghdad* (1924) and *Lost Horizon* (1937).

One of today's best-known Filipino-American actresses is Barbara Luna. Born in New York City to a Filipino father and a Hungarian mother, Barbara made her stage debut at age 11, playing the Polynesian-French daughter of Ezio Pinza in the musical *South Pacific*. She began acting in movies in 1959, usually playing exotic beauties. Her films include *Cry Tough* (1959); *The Devil at 4 O'Clock* (1961); *Ship of Fools* (1965); and *Che!* (1969). In recent years, Barbara Luna has appeared in the daytime TV series "One Life to Live."

Ramon C. Sison, a prominent physician, is also an actor and chairman of the Philippine-American Performing Arts Guild. In 1976, Filipina singer-actress Lita Bennett arranged for Sison to audition for the part of a Filipino doctor in the movie *MacArthur*. He got the part and played a scene with Gregory Peck in the lead role. Other movies followed, including the Golden Globe Award nominee *My Favorite Year* (1983), starring Peter O'Toole. Sison has also made many appearances on television and acted in the plays *A Portrait of the Artist as a Filipino* and *Presence of Mine Enemies.*

Ramon C. Sison (left) and Peter O'Toole in a scene from the movie My Favorite Year

Literature

Carlos Bulosan, who came to Seattle in 1931 as a field worker, is probably the most famous Filipino-American author. Although he died in 1946, some of his books and poems have recently been reprinted, and several biographies of his life are available.

Bulosan's autobiography, *America Is in the Heart,* was a nonfiction best-seller in 1946. This book and other nonfiction works by Bulosan are social protests describing the maltreatment of Filipinos in the United States during the 1930s. This was a subject that the author knew well from his personal experiences in California during this period.

Carlos Bulosan's first book of poems was *Letter from America* (1942), followed by *Chorus for America* (1942), *The Voice of Bataan* (1943), and *The Laughter of My Father* (1944). His poems, articles, and stories also appeared in the *New Yorker, Saturday Review,* and other magazines.

Another award-winning Filipino writer was Evaristo C. Pecson, whose *Bitter Tears of Mother Philippines* was a 1945 best-seller. His book *Our World* received the National Association of Authors and Journalists award in 1947.

In 1977, 12-year-old Melissa Macagba Ignacio wrote *The Philippines: Roots of My Heritage,* based on her year-long stay in the land of her parents. Other Filipino-American writers are

Pacita C. Saludes of Hawaii, who organized GUMIL, or Association of Ilocano Writers, and Marion Caballes, a poet and artist living in New York City. Outstanding newspapermen include Teddy de Nolasco and Benny Evangelista, Jr., a leading reporter for California's *Oakland Tribune*.

Medicine

Perhaps the first Filipino to practice medicine in the United States was Dr. C. T. Blancaflor, who began practicing in Merriman, Nebraska, in 1923. Today, there are thousands of Filipino-American doctors, nurses, dentists, and other medical specialists. Most of them came to the United States after 1965, in the third wave of Filipino immigrants.

One of the busiest and best known is Dr. Ramon C. Sison, a multitalented individual whose career as an actor was described earlier. Dr. Sison is a pathologist, a specialist who studies the causes and symptoms of disease. Since his appointment in 1977 by California Governor Edmund Brown, Jr., he has served on the District 11 Medical Quality Review Committee of the California State Board of Medical Examiners, a group that has the responsibility of watching over the quality of medical care in sprawling Los Angeles County. Dr. Sison has also been president of the Philippine Medical Society of Southern California and a member or leader of many other

Ramon C. Sison not only is a doctor and an actor but also composes music and plays several instruments professionally.

medical, scientific, civic, and military organizations. He helped found and was the first president of the United Filipino-American Assembly of Southern California. Ramon Sison was named 1980-81 "Outstanding Filipino-American" for his civic work.

Lutgarda B. Kuizon is an example of the thousands of dedicated Filipina nurses in the United States. During World War II, she was a nurse with a Filipino guerrilla unit, serving as chief nurse during heavy fighting on the island of Leyte and narrowly escaping capture. After the war, Kuizon came to the United States and obtained a master of arts degree in nursing

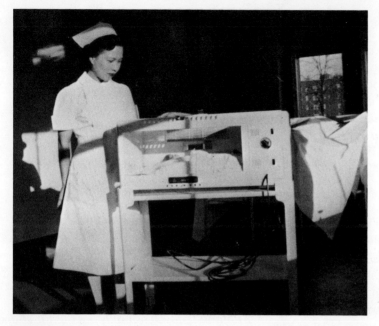

Lutgarda Kuizon watches over a premature baby in the nursery of Columbia Presbyterian Hospital, New York.

administration. She became supervisor of the Pediatrics Department, St. Luke's Hospital, New York, and later was a private nurse caring for cancer patients at the New York and Memorial hospitals in New York City. Even after her retirement in 1980, she nursed infants requiring open-heart surgery.

Examples of the many other Filipino-Americans in medicine are plastic surgeon Ligorio A. Calcacay, Jr., who practices in Pomona, California; neurosurgeon Jesse Schmidt Manlapaz of Danbury, Connecticut; nursing educator Mierfe Tando Calicia of Los Angeles; pharmacist Juanita Cortina Santos of San Diego; J. C. Balcala, an author of nursing books who lives in Scottsburg, Indiana; and Magdalena Pidlaoan-

Vallar of Baltimore, a dentist whose husband, Diggs, constructs dental appliances for her patients.

Science

Most Filipino scientists are newcomers to the United States, but there are several noteworthy names among them.

A Filipino with a skyward gaze, Dr. Eduardo C. San Juan is an aeronautical engineer and advanced projects scientist with Lockheed Corporation. In 1964, he presented one of the first models of a Lunar Roving Vehicle, or "Moon Car." San Juan built his working model from scrap parts and successfully tested it in 1966. Other projects followed, including space shuttle designs, ocean mining vehicles, launch complexes, robots, super cargo trains, and space stations. Presently, he is working on lasers and other high-energy devices.

Among the many unsung Filipino-Americans who have contributed to the U. S. space program are tracking engineer Hermie A. Caballes and quality-control chemist Pedro D. Sarmiento, who uses electronic microscopes to find flaws in spacecraft parts.

Some Filipino-Americans have distinguished themselves in scientific research. Among them is Dr. Aurora V. Revuelta, who came to the United States in the late 1970s as a "balik" or "return" scientist, planning to return to the Philippines after completing her studies. Dr. Revuelta conducted invaluable medical research on the effects of drugs and was named a 1981 Outstanding Filipino Overseas. She eventually married an American and decided to stay in the United States permanently.

A Filipino-American marine biologist, Dr. Mario M. Pamatmat, has measured the oxygen consumption of undersea animals and plants to learn about the possibilities of undersea commercial agriculture and the effects of pollution on underwater life.

The foremost Filipino-American science educator is Dr. Leopoldo V. Toralballa, professor of mathematics at New York University for more than 30 years. A consultant on government projects, he has also written two textbooks, including a 920-page volume on calculus. Toralballa's wife, Dr. Gloria C. Toralballa, is also an outstanding teacher and scientist, serving on the faculty of New York's Hunter College.

Another well-known science educator is Dr. Anastacio L. Palafox, professor of animal science at the University of Hawaii. Dr. Palafox has taught for more than 30 years and has written many scientific articles on animal nutrition, poultry, and agriculture.

Dr. Aurora V. Revuelta came to the United States to study and eventually made her home here.

Dr. Anastacio L. Palafox is a well-known scientist who has received many grants for research in animal nutrition.

Law and Public Service

During *pensionado* days, many Filipinos came to the United States to study law at American universities. Citizenship and other requirements, however, made it impossible for them to practice in some states, especially in the West. One pioneer in the legal profession was Manuel G. Zamora, who, in 1930, became the first Filipino patent attorney in the United States, opening his office in Washington, D.C. Zamora assisted inventors from the Philippines in patenting their inventions in the United States.

The third-wave Filipino immigration after 1965 saw a marked increase in the number of Filipino lawyers and an increase in their professional opportunities as well. In 1977, for example, Wilfrido E. Panote, Jr., became the first Filipino to practice law before the Supreme Court. Today, there are hundreds of Filipino-American lawyers throughout the United States.

Filipino-Americans had entered politics even before the third immigration wave. In 1954, Peter A. Aduja became the first Filipino legislator in Hawaii and perhaps the first in the United States. Hawaii also saw Benjamin Menor become the first state senator in 1962. He is now a member of the

Manuel G. Zamora was one of the first Filipino-Americans to serve in the legal profession.

Benjamin Jerome Cayetano was elected lieutenant-governor of Hawaii in 1986.

In 1970, Filipinos reached a new milestone when California Governor Ronald Reagan appointed Marion Lacadia Obrera as a Los Angeles municipal judge. With this appointment, she became the first U. S. judge of Filipino ancestry.

Sports

Filipino-Americans have had distinguished careers as both amateur and professional athletes. One of the best-known is Tai Babilonia, an outstanding ice skater who was an Olympic competitor.

Born in California to an American mother and a Filipino father who was a detective in the Los Angeles police department, Tai started skating at age seven. At age 9, she was teamed with 11-year-old Randy Gardner. Both youngsters were excellent ice skaters and soon started training with a professional coach. They competed in many regional and national events and in 1976 placed fifth in the Olympics. In 1979, the pair became the first Americans in 29 years to win the World Skating Pairs Championship. They looked like sure winners for the Gold Medal in the 1980 Olympics, but Randy pulled a muscle during training, shattering their hopes for the top honors. Tai went on to become a star with the Ice Capades. She and Randy are still considered among the best American skaters.

Hawaii Supreme Court. Eduardo E. Malapit became the first Filipino elected mayor of an American community (Kauai County, Hawaii, in 1974); he was reelected in 1980.

As of 1986, there were five Filipino mayors and numerous other elected Filipino officials in the United States. Benjamin Jerome Cayetano, who became lieutenant governor of Hawaii on December 1, 1986, was the highest-ranking official of Filipino ancestry in the country. An attorney by profession, Cayetano served 12 years in the Hawaii State Legislature, two terms each in the House and the Senate, before assuming the office of lieutenant governor.

Tai Babilonia and
Randy Gardner

A hopeful for the 1988 Olympics is 16-year-old Susanne Vasquez, the New York State and 1985 National Junior Olympic Tae Kwon Do (Korean karate) champion. Susanne has an excellent chance of making the women's team if the Olympics Committee approves a Tae Kwon Do women's division in 1988. The U. S. Olympic Committee invited her to attend the Olympic Training Center in Boulder, Colorado, in the autumn of 1986 to train under the U. S. Olympic Tae Kwon Do coach.

In an earlier generation, Filipina-American Vicki Manalo Draves won two Gold Medals for diving at the 1948 Olympics in London and later joined the Aqua Follies. Still earlier, Salvador

Susanne Vasquez (left) and Roman Gabriel (above) are two outstanding American athletes of Filipino ancestry.

Cepeda of Chicago was a member of the 1920 Olympic U. S. track and field team.

Roman Gabriel is the best-known professional athlete of Filipino ancestry. He was born in Wilmington, North Carolina, the son of an Irish-American mother and a Filipino immigrant who was a cook on the Atlantic Coast Line Railroad. In high school, Gabriel was a triple-letter winner in sports and an excellent student, receiving about 50 scholarship offers. He chose to attend North Carolina State. The six-foot four-inch, 220-pound "Radar Roman" was NC's all-American quarterback and was drafted by the L. A. Rams in 1962. He was the Rams' All-Pro for 11 years. In 1969, he was named the NFL's "Most Valuable Player" and "Player of the Year." In 1973, Roman Gabriel joined the Philadelphia Eagles and finished his pro career with them in 1975.

Filipino-Americans have also excelled in other professional sports. Bobby Balcena, born in San Pedro, California, played baseball in the 1950s, the only Filipino-American ever to play on a professional baseball team. During his years with the Triple-A Coast League's Seattle Rainiers (1955-1957), he was called the "Filipino Flyer" and was voted the team's "Most Popular Player." After a brief stint with the major-league Cincinnati Reds, Balcena went back to the minors, playing for several different teams until his retirement in 1962.

The first Filipino-American to play professional basketball was Jim Washington, whose parents were born in the Philippines. The six-foot seven-inch forward was drafted in 1965 by the St. Louis Hawks. He was traded to Chicago and Philadelphia, then returned to the Hawks when they moved to Chicago in 1971.

Another Filipino with an American name, Raymond Townsend, played basketball with the Golden State Warriors (Oakland, California) from 1978 to 1980, averaging 5.1 points in 140 games.

Cecilia A. "Ceci" Martinez is the Filipino-American pride in tennis, ranked number one in northern California in 1968 and number 11 nationally in 1969. She won the Philippine Open and the Manila Open in 1970 and later became the head tennis pro at the University Club of Palo Alto, California.

In boxing, there are two top Pinoy names: Bienvenido "Ben" Villaflor, who made World Junior Lightweight Champion in 1972-1977, and Carlos Padilla, Jr., who refereed such famous title fights as Muhammed Ali vs. Joe Frazier, Roberto Duran vs. Sugar Ray Leonard, and Michael Spinks vs. Larry Holmes.

Filipinos display the flag of their native land during an Independence Day parade in Washington, D.C.

There is no question that Filipino-Americans are competitive and always seek excellence in the country they now call home.

INDEX

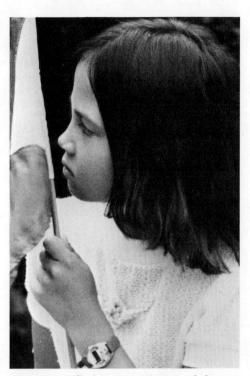

A young Filipina-American celebrates the Fourth of July.

ACKNOWLEDGMENTS The photographs in this book are reproduced through the courtesy of: pp. 2, 39, Library of Congress; pp. 6, 7, 11, 17, 43, Philippine Department of Tourism; p. 9, Philippine Tourist and Travel Association, Inc.; pp. 12, 14, 36, 62 (right), 71, Frank H. Winter; pp. 15, 23 (right), Martin Luther King Library, Washington, D.C.; pp. 18, 26, 49, 61, 66, 69, 70, 72, Alejandrino A. Vincente, Philippine Embassy; pp. 20, 21, 44, 45, 46, National Archives; pp. 23 (left), 28, National Historical Institute, Manila, courtesy of Philippine Embassy; pp. 25, 27, Reuters/Bettmann Newsphotos; p. 31, Special Collections, Gelman Library, George Washington University; p. 32, National Air and Space Museum; pp. 34, 35, Hawaii State Archives; p. 40, University of Washington; p. 41, Rufino Cacabelos; pp. 50, 56 (left), Reynaldo Alejandro; p. 51, Val M. Laigo; p. 52, José Aruego; p. 53, Evelyn Mandac; p. 54, Michael Dadap; p. 55, Philippine Dance Company; p. 56 (right), Atlanta Ballet; p. 57, Filipino Youth Activities, Seattle; pp. 58, 59, Ramon C. Sison; p. 60, Lutgarda B. Kuizon; p. 62, Dr. Anastacio L. Palafox; p. 63, Office of the Lieutenant Governor, Hawaii; p. 64, Michael Levine Public Relations Co.; p. 65 (left), Susanne Vasquez; p. 65 (right), Los Angeles Rams.

Front cover photograph: Filipino Youth Activities, Seattle. Back cover photographs: University of Washington (left); Atlanta Ballet (upper right); Office of the Lieutenant Governor, Hawaii (lower right).

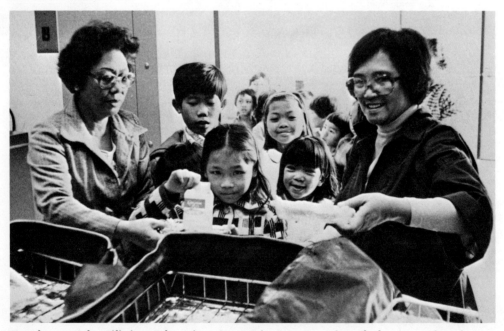

Teachers at the Filipino Education Center in San Francisco help young immigrants from the Philippines to learn English and adapt to American life.

FRANK H. WINTER is an Assistant Curator in the Space Science and Exploration Department at the Smithsonian Institution's National Air and Space Museum in Washington, D.C. While his professional life has been devoted to the study of spaceflight, Winter has long had a deep personal interest in the Philippines and its people. He is married to a Filipina, the former Fe Dulce Kuizon Rosal, who is a descendant of the 16th-century Filipino leader Lapu-Lapu. In his many visits to the Philippines, Winter has studied the archipelago's varied culture and the forces that impelled Filipinos to emigrate to the United States. This book, his second for young readers, is a product of that research. His publications for adults include numerous articles and several books about the history of rocketry and spacefight.

Born in England, Frank Winter now lives in Burke, Virginia, with his wife and two children.

THE *IN AMERICA* SERIES

AMERICAN IMMIGRATION
THE **AMERICAN INDIAN,** VOL. I
THE **AMERICAN INDIAN,** VOL. II
THE **ARMENIANS**
THE **BLACKS**
THE **CHINESE**
THE **CZECHS & SLOVAKS**
THE **DANES**
THE **DUTCH**
THE **EAST INDIANS & PAKISTANIS**
THE **ENGLISH**
THE **FILIPINOS**
THE **FINNS**
THE **FRENCH**
THE **GERMANS**
THE **GREEKS**
THE **HUNGARIANS**

THE **IRISH**
THE **ITALIANS**
THE **JAPANESE**
THE **JEWS**
THE **KOREANS**
THE **LEBANESE**
THE **MEXICANS**
THE **NORWEGIANS**
THE **POLES**
THE **PUERTO RICANS**
THE **RUSSIANS**
THE **SCOTS & SCOTCH-IRISH**
THE **SWEDES**
THE **UKRANIANS**
THE **VIETNAMESE**
THE **YUGOSLAVS**

Lerner Publications Company
241 First Avenue North · Minneapolis, Minnesota 55401